OUR WAYS ON EARTH

By the same author:

OUR WAYS ON EARTH

PETER BAKOWSKI

RECENT
WORK
PRESS

Our Ways on Earth
Recent Work Press
Canberra, Australia

Copyright © Peter Balowski, 2022

ISBN: 9780645180879 (paperback)

A catalogue record for this
book is available from the
National Library of Australia

Cover image: © Ophelia Bakowski
Author photograph: © Andrew Bott
Cover design: Ophelia Bakowski with Recent Work Press
Set by Recent Work Press

recentworkpress.com

For Helen and Ophelia Bakowski

Contents

'A painter told me that nobody could draw a tree without in some sort becoming a tree...'

\- Ralph Waldo Emerson

Driving instructions

Start the poem with a verb,
release the handbrake that's a comma,
but slow for the intersection of two thoughts.

Once you know where the poem is going,
accelerate before it gets dark.

Stay alert to changing conditions—
soft edges, metaphors bounding across the road,
falling rocks strewn in your path by an internal critic.

Upon reaching the destination, try to accept that it may not be
the destination which you had in mind,
but that's poetry for you.
Check that your licence for it
hasn't expired.

Poem to the pencil

Please, when you feel not much more than a stub, know that the
Eraser is your friend, ready to follow you anywhere. And the
Notebook will always greet you with open arms. I
Cherish each shopping list and recipe you've helped me write out
In all kinds of weather. You're magical, more than wood and lead.
Let's wander, beyond the backs of envelopes, underlining as we go.

Ode to water

Drip, leak, puddle, river, lake, ocean—
not always pacific, at times terrifying admirals and plumbers,
you're forgiven by the thirsty who raise their glasses to you.

Often you escape the clumsy—
spill from pitcher, bucket, waiter's tray. It's hard to retain you.
Your wish is to be liquid music, which you often are
when you announce yourself as rain.

Portrait of Lucian Freud in his studio, Kensington, London, 9 December 2004

The individuals I paint—some lie splayed,
arranged across the floorboards, washed up against a reef
of cleaning rags, a shore of skirting board.
Some have stumbled their way here
from thorn and thistle railway cuttings,
the cat corpse alleys of London,
bang their fists on my door.

I guide them down the hallway to the studio,
anchor them in a leather chair with a whiskey,
select paintbrushes, the colours necessary
to render each skeletal or abundant body.

I dance around the canvas, jab at the canvas,
the palette more talisman than shield,
locked in my fight against repetition,
to thrill myself with paint.

I have lived an unconstrained life.
Painting. Sex. Gambling.
In pursuing each
I've hurt, diminished, repelled
friends, lovers, family, innocents.

Loss leaves me stripped,
raw enough to go further with portraiture.
I'm unapologetic,

accept it all, every hue of laceration,
as I look at myself in the studio mirror,
study the autumn of my face.

Portrait of Philip Larkin, November 1977

I begin another letter to Monica—
work with adjective and noun, complaint and conjunction,
and at the risk of injuring the recipient,
hurl the hand grenade of an indelicate statement
about marriage and children—
how the reality of either would attack
my solitude, the valued quiet.

Yet, whenever I write the words,
'I should...'
the search begins
for a less fearful me
who would complete that sentence.
I sense he's there,
outside the margins of a poem.

Being selfish, unfaithful, dutiful, supportive, morbid, witty—
these are my traits—some inoperable, some conscience-sprung.
Too many nights I do what is easier—avoid the blank page,
return to comforting tasks—
the shelving of a book,
the washing of a cup and saucer.

In this ordered room,
I sit until the last afternoon schoolboy passes,
running a stick against iron fence railings.
Then I pour myself an Irish whiskey,
make a phone call to my doctor
who's keen on ballroom dancing, not poetry.

Portrait of Graham Greene, 1952

Drinking a second martini at The Hatted Chicken,
I hear talk of war breaking out in other lands.
Back in my hotel room, I trace those contours in an atlas,
consider which newspaper will pay me to venture there,
whether tonight a Nembutal capsule or prayer
will help me sleep.

Saigon, city of heat and mistrust.
I'm learning to infiltrate or eavesdrop,
to blend into an arcade's protective shadow
or move surely through a barrage of peddlers
desperate to sell me
saucy postcards, a snakeskin wallet, a ballpoint pen.

In bars of varied repute, I steer conversations,
buy shots of bourbon and cognac, rivers of beer
for pilots, soldiers, surveyors, detonation experts.
I listen, separate brag from slipped fact,
practise my smile in the barroom mirror—
a wince, some would call it.
My safety is temporary,
I'm a straw man waiting for the next typhoon.

Meanwhile I write—500 words a day.
An image or an utterance
scaffolds a paragraph or scene,
reveals a character
perhaps vengeful with their ledger of grudges,

never leaving fingerprints
or a living witness.

Opium—release from all my disguises.
Flame. Ember. Ash.
I call for another pipe.
Time. Love. Hate. They hold no tyranny.
Flame. Ember. Ash.
My distant wife—her silhouette there
amongst the curtains, fades
and I'm alone,
reaching for a glass of water
and then my hat—
another Englishman
descending illicit stairs
into foreign heat.

The frozen borderline
- for Nico

The sweep of searchlights.
Silhouettes running. Gunfire.

I know what the morning light will show—
corpses in the fields,
their shoes already stolen.

In the sky,
more locust bombers—
the bridges and shunting yards
their choice harvest.

Those who run the world,
ruin the world.

Choir of widows,
choir of orphans,
sing your songs
in the empty market square
between the cathedral and the abattoir.

Homeless man in winter, Collins Street, Melbourne, 2019

Turn up your collar against the
Hailstone judgements of passersby. Some give your
Existence, the slump of you, wide berth.

Coroner wind scours an alley, prods at an
Overdose. The ambulance driver doesn't bother with the siren, having
Abandoned his search for a pulse. The sun's a coin, rolls down
The drain, out of reach—but there are still two buttons on your coat.

Diary entries in the year 2020

Here in Melbourne all playgrounds are closed.
Council workers aren't painting the town red.
The sound of one hand clapping has been replaced
by the sound of two hands being washed.

This long April I opened the world atlas.
My index finger follows a shipping lane across the Pacific
to San Francisco and back.
I don't get seasick, forget to buy postcards,
but I spy some flying fish—
there they are—caught in the dusty curtains.

Where you aren't
may appear more alluring than where you are—
but that could change tomorrow.

I think of those who used to mingle,
knock over glasses of wine at smoke-thick parties—
now attempting to read Proust,
pausing to consider where in their backyard
they'll grow tomatoes next spring,
prepared to dirty their knees,
stab at the earth with a spade—
vigilant for the first glimmer of green,
for the vulnerable to become sturdy.

I listen to Radio National.

Disparate voices and viewpoints. Science and speculation.
The latest statistics, the different scenarios—
what's possible, what's probable.
Facts and fallacies. Hygiene and hysteria.
The economy, that poor performer,
may be dragged from centre stage.

Worry—that horse with three legs.
I try to practise gratitude
here under this cat-traipsed roof
far from New York City, former stomping ground of
Lou Reed, Ted Berrigan, William Burroughs—
phrase detectives in search of the killer line.

Cautious morning dog walks in Barkly Gardens.
Passing others at the recommended distance.
The occasional ripple of a smile.
Optimism, pessimism—I'm not immune to either
in this day-by-day world.

The sky is itself again, bird-won—planes
grounded, hem the perimeter of Tullamarine airport.
Adjust your appetites to what's unread on the bookshelf—
perhaps *A Country in the Moon*, a travel book on Poland.

History remains big-themed—
exploration and genocide, plague and science, trauma and art.
Our existence—threatened, questioned, perhaps undeserved,
is discussed again in essays and debate,
no conclusions drawn,
only further caricatures of our leaders.

These weeks—adjusting, adapting to containment,
monitoring my body, each impulse.
I'm alive—a privilege, a gift,
but I haven't shouted my thanks up and down the street.

I look out the front window.
I can't see the future,
I see the trees,
stripped of their brittle armour.

Take a deep breath

A crisis brings to light what's important, what may need to be
Sacrificed for the greater good. Debate continues as to which is the
Priority—our health or the economy? Meanwhile many are glad to
Inhale and exhale. Millions have been removed from
Routine, employment and industry. The world has been
Altered, our ailments exposed. It's time for deep scrutiny and
Thought concerning our actions, methods and motives and their
Implications—who they affect, who benefits. Let's foster a code of
Openness, generosity towards each other, to realise our human
Need for safety, education and tolerance—a vision that's inclusive not
Selective, which marks us as a community.

Backwater song

Mindy didn't leave a note.

She once mentioned a cousin in Philly but he might be a lie.
Anyway I can't make the bus fare.

Sitting on the porch, I'm alert
to movement slithering fatal in the bayou reeds
or the pigeon-toed approach of Floyd Hammit
with his beer belly and dented sheriff's badge,
ready to bellow a howdy through the screen door.

Around a decade ago Floyd crossed the colour line,
lay with Mindy in that abandoned shack on Firefly Hill,
the one in which Hal Giltrebb hung himself.

When Floyd's ailing wife, Mary Ann, died from tuberculosis
Floyd drank a Mississippi of beer—
jury in his head calling for punishment.
One night, neighbours heard a gunshot in Floyd's house.
Hell, he was ashamed of that bullet hole in the bedroom wall.
For a while I wished that Floyd was a better shot
but that kind of thinking made me feel lower than a turtle's belly.

I prayed a little, fished a little,
tension eased in my shoulders
and I put my mind
into my harmonica playing,
sitting out each night on the cooling porch—
mixing notes in with frog, cricket and grasshopper sounds
until I was more spirit than man.

This year Floyd and I have gone forwards—
talk about favourite baseball pitchers and Dixieland tunes,
how both of us don't always like to study ourselves in the mirror
first thing in the morning,
how some fish you catch are poisonous,
need to be thrown back in the water.
Sometimes there's laughter, a game of chess,
two men quiet
when a bishop or a knight is moved.

Without a safety net

It began with Father taking Petra to see the Russian circus—
necks craned to marvel at the tightrope walker,
her sequinned leotard, measured steps.

It's ending in a palliative care ward in Studley Park Road,
far from Moscow, the year of training with Gypsy Ivan.

The drumroll evenings under the big top. Sawdust, popcorn,
thunderous applause in all the toured cities.
Lisbon, Athens, New York City—
recalled sights now awash with morphine.

Monica, the attending nurse
looks at her watch.
Another 30 minutes until the shift finishes.
In her apartment she'll kick off her shoes,
search the internet again for other work,
something in hospitality…

Petra has visitors—
a neighbour, a cousin. Once a week, a priest.
He talks of mercy.

Someone has removed Petra's wedding ring.

Beyond the sterile room
church bells toll,
a lawn mower is heard
and the barking of a dog.

In the bush, north of Buchan

So you've fled the city, its enslaved traffic, clogged
Arteries, to sit on a tree stump, eat pink wedges of watermelon,
No longer wear shoes. Tonight the crescent moon is the first to be
Coaxed onto the celestial dancefloor. Its partner, a gallant star. From
The vicinity of the pond, several green vocalists pipe
Up, largely baritones. As the evening unfurls, some
Ambitious solos are taken. Round midnight you decide it's time to
Retire, though a wristwatch is something you no longer have up
Your sleeve.

Isolated cottage off Gelantipy Road

Ron's 1964 white Ford sedan is a good ol' girl,
chugs along, has moss on her rear fender.
The upholstery's shot, tufts of yellow foam rubber showing.

The car aerial's a wire coat hanger
and the fuel cap disappeared years ago.
A scrunched-up souvenir tea towel does the job.

Ron's on a pension.
Four slices of white bread with blackberry jam for breakfast,
washed down with cups of strong black tea.
Often a bit of kangaroo from the freezer for dinner.
Boiled potatoes on the side.

Single bed. Blanket has a couple of cigarette burns.
Car parts on the kitchen table. Fan belt. Carburettor. Spark plugs.

Ron's Mum died young when he was in kindergarten.
His Dad married again—a Polish woman who Ron has never liked.
Christmas now. It's Ron and Thommo, his black Labrador.
They both have two lamb chops for Christmas lunch—
raw for Thommo, well-grilled for Ron.

The scarecrow

Straw-stuffed custodian. Some say that you lack ambition.
Button-eyed, tearless—you let the rain do all your weeping
and the wind all your rambling.
Couch spring ribs, broomstick spine, table leg arms,
you cannot repulse drought, flood, an onslaught of locusts.
You stand there as a field mouse, skittish in the pale dawn,
inspects a furrow.

Beneficiary

Far below the hairpin bend
a fox drinks rainwater
from an upturned hubcap.

Surrealist weather report

When it rains it purrs.

Mission update

'Celesta, I can see the outline of Australia through the viewfinder.
Get ready. Recharge the electric lasso
and make sure you pack the *long* extension cord.'

'Wait, Galacto, have you ever lassoed a kangaroo?'

'Can't say that I've ever lassoed any critter.
Certainly not a bouncy one.'

'Hmm, I think we'd better re-watch some Westerns,
see how it's done. Do kangaroos *stampede* like buffalo?'

'Er, Celesta, the DVD player's not working…'

'Lordy, what an assignment. I need a drink.
How far is it to the nearest old skool bar, Galacto?'

'Neptuna told me about this place
called The Dapper Rabbit in Melbourne—
inner city hipster crowd
but ordinary Joes and Janes drink there too.
The matter transmitter cubicle… indicates…
it'll take us 4 seconds to get there.'

'Is there a dress code, Celesta?'

'No, Nep' said it's casual.
Plus they have a wide range of craft beers
and Fridays, there's a DJ spinning Yacht Rock Classics—

Boz Scaggs, Sade, Doobie Brothers, Hall & Oates.'

'It sounds good, Celesta. Really good.'

Brenda and Steffi at The Dapper Rabbit, 2 July 2021

'Brenda, there's something about that couple.
Yeah, those two at the back corner table.
I'm picking up an *aura*. Vibrations. Energy.
Some sort of latent power…'

'Aw C'mon, Steffi. Relax.
I know what it is. You've had your nose into those weird books
you bought from The Theosophical Society Bookshop—
reiki, crop circles, the Bavarian Illuminati, white magic.
My motto is 'Go with what you know'
and for me that's getting plastered here on Friday night.
I always remain ladylike though I may tilt a little
and not be up for a game of Scrabble.'

'No, I'm serious, Brenda. Their eyes. They're set too far apart
and *why* are both of them wearing mittens? It's not that cold.
At first I thought undercover cops but I can't see any holster bulge,
plus they're not fidgety or giving off a macho vibe.
In fact they're kind of sexless.'

'Maybe, they're clergy, Steffi. Born in some backwater part
of Ireland. They look pale enough. If you read your
Graham Greene you'll find some priests slurping and spilling
whiskey, to be sure, to be sure.'

'Sorry Brenda, but those two are giving me the heebie-jeebies.
I'm going to slip into the Ladies and have some Rescue Remedy.'

'You do that Steffi. I'll stay here and drink for both of us. I've got a lot to forget.'

Up against the ropes

The chateau is understaffed.
The cook, Claudette, quit without notice,
claimed that the aftershave, used by Bernard the kitchenhand,
made her eyes water, caused her to sneeze into the saucepans.
Harry suggests that it's a good time
for us to embark on a 5 day fast.

I've enrolled at the gym. Boxing lessons.
Matteo my personal trainer
has already complimented me on my balance.
Must be all those ballet lessons I endured.

During boxing sessions, Matteo does seem to touch me a lot.
'Well, it is a contact sport,' he says,
while kneeling in front of me to adjust my hips.
'The ability to swivel and thrust. So important.'

I think Harry may be having an affair. He's dressing better.
Wearing shirts with cufflinks and the other day I smelt aftershave.
Rummaging through the dresser drawers,
looking for a bowtie, *not* looking at me, Harry said,

'Well Bernard gave me a bottle to try. Says he buys it in bulk.
There's the equivalent in perfume for women. It's called *Advance*.
Hey, I'm taking the Merc. I'll be back from Zurich as soon as I can.
Give Miranda a call. She's always up for some shopping.'

I wanted to say to Harry, 'Shopping's not everything,'
but I held back.

Portrait of happiness

for Connie Bensley

Hints of you appear
in children playing pavement hopscotch,
the parcel-laden woman offered a seat on the bus,
the homing pigeon breeder releasing a cooing favourite
into the abiding air.
Today the sun warms each considerate hand
tending to pot plants, modest gardens, the shifting of a
caterpillar.
The end of the world will have to wait or else slip into a cafe
for a currant bun—the ones with vanilla icing are the best.

Arthur reveals his thoughts and plans to Wendy

If you were a lion-tamer
you wouldn't want to smell meaty.
Two showers a day would be best.

With the help of Uncle Des
I've composed some lion-pleasing music—
drums with lots of splashing noises using
a bucket of water and the toilet plunger
to remind my lion of his favourite watering hole in Namibia,
brimming with hippos and flamingos.

My lion wouldn't sleep in a cage.
He'd sleep by my bed.
I'd be careful not to step on him
If I needed to go to the bathroom
in the middle of the night.

I've saved up twelve pounds towards buying my lion.
Mum and Dad think I'm saving up to buy a new pushbike.
Parents can be clueless sometimes.

Collage portrait of Joseph Cornell, inspired by his jottings on napkins and envelopes

Hunched over my workbench, my altar of trial and error,
I assemble box after box
in which I may choreograph the placement of
a marble, a skate key, an engraving of a finch, a photo of Debussy—
seek via enclosure to disclose affinities between
a swan's neck and the question mark,
a gramophone needle and an anteater's snout.

A compass, a jade thimble, a steamship ticket,
drawers full of glass eyes and whales' teeth,
suggest voyages, adventures, destinies,
fortify me in mother-shadowed rooms.

I escape to the ballet, watch the dancers
fluent-limbed within the spotlight's circle.
After the performance, on the train ride home,
I recall their costumes, leaps and pirouettes,
their bodies' obedience,
plan the allegorical homage I'll stage
within the image constellation of a box.

Each box is an invitation—to enter
a room, a desert, a belltower,
share an apple with a prince,
drink water from the same stream as a unicorn.
When I finally agree to a gallery exhibiting my work,
my reward isn't the critics' praise,

but to see a child let go of their parent's hand
to pause at each box,
come away beguiled
with a volley of questions.

Once upon a time the great seas were uncharted,
once upon a time my father was alive—
together we watched the circus strongman,
bare-chested, break free of every binding chain.
I applauded until my hands were raw.

Sundays I sit in Bickford's.
The pleated glass of a sugar dispenser,
the amber hair clasp worn by a waitress,
the tines of my cake fork,
become moments which I re-spool,
will revere again in the bachelor dark.

I live, but at a distance from participation—
a reader of history and furtive glances.
Out on the periphery, I sift through
junk stores, what others have discarded.
I'll die in my protective shell—
perhaps a last, unfinished collage
there on the workbench,
a puzzle of allusions
for one of my assistants to study,
then boldly complete.

Portrait of a lone diner at a restaurant in Chelsea

How you are
that's what matters or what's the matter—
whether you're
right in the head,
left in your head
or ahead of yourself,
allergic to shellfish and the selfish,
wanting to see the menu again.

But the sole waiter
has his head in the clouds…
You bite your tongue,
hide under the table,
admire the legs of other tables…

and a great distance remains
between you and the mastery
of yourself and the evening.

Acceptance

To live alone, far from cities, market square gossip,
has been Jeanne's way since she left Lyon at the age of
seventeen.

Her income is steady. Jeanne has regular customers—
one, a retired admiral, who lives in Dakar,
buys, every second month, via mail order,
several hundred euros of her essences and herbal cures.

Her days are ones of study—soil, moisture and mineral levels,
root systems, vital and parasitic insects…
Last month Jeanne drove into Carcassonne—
a meeting with her lawyer—a final adjustment to her will.

She's bequeathed her house and its extensive grounds to the
province,
envisages children pausing at the Dolphin fountain,
testing with a finger, the temperature of the water,
then walking hushed down the shaded avenue of oaks,
to delight in the Butterfly House.

Tremors again in Jeanne's right hand.
Feeling weak she climbs the stairs, lies on the bed.
Fever. Hallucinations. The frightening sensation
of each limb being gnawed.
The legacy of her two bouts of malaria in Indochine—
there to collect plant specimens.
Beyond the open bedroom window bees are heard,
sudden among the spring flowers.

The ache

Christos hopes to sell his last jars
of red capsicum at the Friday market.
Gina will be there
at the stall next to his,
with her baskets of Spanish onions and yellow lemons.

Some speculation about the weather,
what the boat from Piraeus may bring
and Christos will feel again
too unpractised to talk further,
busy himself among his jars,
dust each lid needlessly,
the cloth, a small white flag of surrender.

The purse

It's scuffed and the zipper gets a bit stuck.
The current contents—
a bus ticket to Canvey Island,
three crumpled IOUs from Sonja, an ex-flatmate,
and a tube of pink lipstick
nicked from Selfridges.

Not enough weight in it
to throw at Eric
who's only ever bought me
a pregnancy test kit.

He *still* hasn't phoned.
I felt the first kick yesterday.

Bath time

Beyond the kneecap islands
an archipelago of toes can been seen,
one recently stubbed.

A sea shanty is sung
into a shampoo bottle microphone.

The fin of a washcloth
passes on the starboard side.

The soap remains lost
beneath the clotted waves—
it was last seen
entering a cove,
perhaps indecent to name.

An actor eclipsed
- for Hugo Williams

In a last good suit, Tony bellows 'Not now!'
at each child and a big-footed debt collector,
wipes perspiration from his brow with a white cotton
handkerchief,
a smear of scarlet lipstick in its monogrammed corner.

A Muggsy Spanier 78 blares from the gramophone.
The trumpet solo frightens the cat, wakes Melissa,
hungover and askew in the gardener's cottage.

Perhaps the market will bear
a second volume of autobiography, racy in parts...

Nowadays Tony is ferried to the doctor's more often than
somewhere select for lunch.

Portrait of Caetano Veloso, London, December 1971

Brazil and my sister's face—
each day I find them harder to summon.
Cry me a river, make it the Amazon.

English words and phrases. Short sharp darts—
Pint. Snog. Tiff. Daft. Lark. Bonk.
Pulling your leg. Cat got your tongue?
Language is a tightrope.
I fall bruised to Chelsea pavements.

Writing songs—I study wallpaper roses,
dive into mirrors,
ganja-float in bedroom galaxies.
Sometimes the Notting Hill streets are snow-clenched,
sometimes they're groovy.

My fraying disguises,
I watch them tumble dry
in the all-night laundrette.

How long does a sentence last?
Ask each poet and songwriter,
ask every regime.

Portrait of Syd Barrett

No quiet study of a trio of willows
by the unspooled River Cam.
Under London skies there's pressure
to produce another hit single,
but you began in art,
pop goes the easel.

Swallow a tab,
orbit the wallpaper solar system.
You plummet back to Earth
towards a glass of water,
a few crumbs of sleep.
Raindrops worm their way
across the floorboards.

Ice cream. Muesli.
The girls loved loosely.
Postcards and letters
fall through the slot.
Some can't be answered,
ask too much,
bruise the adored.

Octopus lad, avoid the net and the prod,
the shadows of hulls above you.
Perhaps you can dive
into the moon-strummed waves
of a children's book.

Withdrawal from the scene.

Back to Cambridge—
not a penance,
but a need.

You slump on the couch, come apart,
turn inwards, except for little errands—
groceries, garden and art supplies, hardware.

Your painter's eye and hand,
guided to the more—
what's there beneath the sheen and story
of tangled lovers, the vase of violets capsized by their bed,
the open window where leaping's done.
Your shapes and symmetries are not ill.

A still life is still a life.

Work created,
work destroyed.
Decisions—yours to avoid or make.
Sister and brothers and friends visit gingerly
with their whys in a knot.

You walk away
from all the ruffled feathers and daughters,
into your room,
not cell but sanctuary.

There's the cross-legged study of each floorboard,
thoughts and cigarette smoke rise,

become wisps,
then less.

No more your confinement
in the zoo of songs.

Blind Joe's Creek

Joe bends to the sound of flowing water, drinks his fill.

High in the gums magpies warble.

Maybe in the next life
Joe will have wings, safe places to perch…

Joe hears the snapping of twigs,
hopes it's kangaroos not coppers.

He remembers a prayer from the orphanage,
the softer voice of Sister Agnes
who'd check his hair for lice.

Being alone,
away from bed wetting and beatings,
that's the only way.

Joe lies low in the tall grass, listens again—
there are no troubling sounds.

A farm. He senses there's one nearby—
He'd trod in some cow dung
a while earlier.
Well, that's better than
stepping into a rabbit trap.

In Shangri La

The mist is a child,
plays hide and seek
with the mountains.

The women collect wild berries—
red treasure amongst the pines,
sing on the forest path home.

The arrow-maker sits on a stool
tamps tobacco into his pipe.
He has never left this valley
of ample barley and firewood.

Winter is coming
to test our blood and faith.

There'll be hunger, deaths,
weeping and ritual.

Little is known,
much is loved.

The court decides

The drunk fisherman, seaweed for a pillow,
the jealous husband, quick with the knife,
each has sullied his name.

They'll be made
to carry sacks of copra to the trading station,
haul water from the forest spring.
May their exertions be penance.

Each evening
the sorcerer will smear herbs and charcoal
across their foreheads
to rid them of ill thoughts
sown by demons.

When the moon is again a curved blade
the two men will be allowed
to sleep and eat within a day's walk of the
village,
and should be granted
every courtesy.

Oh human traveller

Watch out for
leeches
bandits
malaria
altitude sickness
mutiny amongst the porters
frostbite
avalanches.

Learn
the language
the customs
when to leave
by foot
by horseback
by backroads
at night.

Endure
the blizzards
the dust storms
the perilous mountain
ascent
descent
the navigation of rapids.

Be astounded
by the vistas
palaces

fortresses
shamans
oracles
the stubbornness
of mules and bureaucrats.

May you shed unwanted
possessions
burdens
coldness
learn from rituals and ways of being
you've witnessed,
have begun to practise.

The very rich hours
- for Freddie Spencer Chapman

Time—that gruff commander, never sits on his hands.
Hesitancy is a form of foul weather.
Endeavor is the answer. Hit the high, exhilarating road,

Past all opposition. Leave the naysayers behind.
Reward lies in flora and fauna, new to the eye. Plateaux await your
Enthralled, dogged crossing. A pause is allowed. You may wish to
Survey your attire as you reach each pinnacle, a personal Mount
Everest, rigorous in your pursuits. To do, to exult in the
Now, enables you to maintain your distance from the tremulous, the
Tentative, who fail to drag you down to their dispiriting level.

Checking in

Change challenges, impels us to ingenuity and invention—
from the carrier pigeon to the telegram,
from the fax machine to the Zoom meeting.

To talk and listen, air ideas and perceptions,
to consider and respond
and advance conversationally outside the realms of work,
to chat about families, sport, the book one's reading—
these courtesies may establish common ground,
encourage further analysis,
reveal or suggest what must be understood to proceed.

Our relationships, new and established, are our teachers, our
currency,
remind us with each phone call or email
of the value and trust inherent in sharing news
and perhaps our deepest concerns.

Wider human contact began through the language of drums—
this reaching out beyond the known
is our story, our parable, which may grant us guidance
through each unfolding day.

Consider your purpose

Perhaps your purpose is to
temper an ego, restore balance and reason,
illuminate a new path.

Let our belief in process and rigour
send us into library, laboratory and conference.

Let history and our conscience remind us
to be vigilant and honourable
in the use of our learning and influence
as we seek to make the world attentive
to its glories and challenges.

A sculptor interrupted

Hammer blows then curses issue from Damien's shed.
The NO ENTRY sign which hangs from the door
is ignored daily by one or more of the children.

Today two of them want a dispute settled—
'Wendy's had the slingshot for *an hour*, it's my turn now…'

Still holding the chisel and hammer
Damien surveys Arthur's tear-streaked face…
'Go see your mother.
I'm trying to get the nose right on this lady. She became a saint,
which is unlikely for either of you…'

'I want to be a pilot.'
'I want to be a ballerina.'

'Well, you'll have to do your homework.'

'I've got *really* good eyesight,
spot rabbits hopping in the meadow before anyone else.'

'And I've got long arms and legs. I can reach Mum's hatbox
without using the footstool.'

'Well, you'll still have to do your homework.'

'You've already said that Dad.'

'That's true. True as the big bucket of potatoes in the kitchen which need peeling right now. Your mother will give each of you a knife, maybe a scone with jam after. Better than homework, right? Off you go. I'm glad that's sorted. Now back to that nose…'

Observing Buzz, a black miniature poodle

Bone archaeologist,
urine philanthropist,
pat collector,
your nose is a workaholic.

But then you'll sleep,
recharge the batteries in your tail, that sure indicator
of how you feel about
those approaching
furred, friendly or furtive.

The contents of your food bowl
must align with your belly,
be up to scratch.

The pianist

When I'm grown
and have memorised the latitude and longitude
of the world's major cities,
I'll become a pilot,
head straight for the equator,
which is like the leather belt
Uncle Des wears to hold up his Sunday trousers
when he visits to borrow money from Dad, to bet on horses—
Lemon Flower, Intangible, Likely Lad.

Poor Uncle Des.
The lenses on his spectacles are so thick.
He could never have been a pilot.

On each visit
he'll sit down at the piano in our parlour,
shoo the cat away from the foot pedals.

Then he stares at the keys for ages,
calls it 'summoning'.

Strange music. Great gobs of time between notes.
Not many notes either.
Each finger hovers above the keys,
like a bee choosing between flowers.

It's usually me who sees Uncle Des to the door.
I watch him amble up Smythe Hill,
stop to study the bark of a tree,

a white butterfly on a fence post.

He walks like his music.

Dog walk

It's agreeable, this walkabout ritual—
the zig zag investigation of each smell,
adding the postscript of our own canine contribution.

The hands of the town hall clock pin clouds to the sky.
The sun lifts its head from the book of the horizon.
Abandoned shopping trolleys lie on their silver sides
in Cameron Street.

A white flag hasn't been raised
but rather a poo bag—
let us bend to our task,
carry this biodegradable trophy
to the nearest bin.

Today, there aren't witnesses with approving smiles,
only three construction cranes in the distance
conveying heavier loads.

Work, rest and play

Arthur has a wooden sword and,
pretending to limp, a wooden leg.
He cries out a lament to anyone within earshot—
'A chest of gold doubloons lost overboard in that storm…'

'Fetch that keg of rum!' he commands Wendy.
Wendy has set out her plastic tea set,
asks a one-eyed doll,
'Another cup of tea, Miss Adler?'

'You'll be walking the plank soon, Wendy…'

'A slice of marble cake, Mr Jenkins?'

Arthur throws his sword into the fishpond,
is sulking hard beneath the willow tree.
He has four marbles in his trouser pockets.
The tear in the left knee is new.
Arthur will tell Mum it happened in Sherwood Forest,
when he was engaged in a battle with Count Drago of Essex.

Arthur likes to watch his Mum sew and mend.
The needle dives beneath the cloth,
then surfaces, rises, dives again,
near the island of a button.

While Mum sews, they have a humbug each
and soon it's evening
with the sound of Dad removing his boots at the door

and Meadow the cat allowed to come inside
to settle where no-one will disturb her until morning.

Portrait of our next-door neighbour

B is for Bernard
who's rather scarred.
Spry but shy, he may be glimpsed
weeding his armpits in the backyard.

He drives a hearse
which he has no wish to fill
with passengers living, dead or ill.

Bernard once had a mother
but he swapped her for another,
cleaner and younger.
On Sundays they play badminton
or throw kittens back and forth to each other.

A person of no harmful ambition,
Bernard sits in his cane chair
and embroiders cushions.
The movement of needle and thread
keeps his mind off Dreidel,
his last wife who fell on a knife
while cleaning the glass leaves of a chandelier.

Bernard claimed to be in Yorkshire at the time. Birdwatching.
In court, he produced a blurred photo of a startled meadowlark.

Sgt Snout of the local constabulary
is pressing to reopen the case.

All the colours of the rainbow

Arthur picks up the snail from the middle of the gravel road,
places it in the grass.
Besides snails Arthur likes words and geography.
Currently the class is learning about New Zealand.
One day Arthur would like to go there,
preferably without his sister Wendy,
who is a sticky beak, a snitch, a sook and most likely, a thief—
one of Arthur's Derwent pencils is missing, the crimson one.

When quizzed about its whereabouts Wendy said that
a few nights ago, she'd heard this whirring sound in the
backyard,
louder than Dad's ride-on mower,
figured it was a spaceship landing,
but didn't tell Arthur about it, didn't want to scare him
as he's such a bed-wetter…

Wendy didn't get any further with her
aliens landing perhaps on the hunt for Derwent pencils story
as Arthur who *hadn't* wet the bed for 19 nights straight
punched Wendy in the nose.

Wendy went running down the hallway,
blood dripping on the new Axminster carpet.

Mum was on the phone to one of the school Mums…
Now there was blood on her apron
as Wendy buried her face in its folds.

'Excuse me Suzanne, I'm afraid I'll have to get off the phone.
There's been a little, er, incident here. I'm sure it's nothing.
You know children…
I'll ring you back about cakes for the school fete. 'bye for now.'

Poem to a spider

Bulbous weaver,
your legs are compass points
which guide you to the wreckage of a fly—
delectable wings and fuselage
splayed across your web.

Your numerous eyes watch
the stockinged housekeeper
with her raised slipper—
one accurate slap may
reduce you to a smear.

You have no armour,
only the sanctuary of a crack,
in this house,
where at all hours
the tenant calls out
her husband's name.

Jennifer talks to Glenda, her neighbour

Wendy has hidden the dishwashing liquid again.
Last time I found it in the woodshed.
She doesn't know that Damien and I have decided
to send her to a boarding school.

There will be tears on both sides but it's necessary.
Damien says he needs to concentrate.
This commission could lead to bigger things—
his sculptures in other public places,
even overseas.

I've never cooked with prunes before.
It's a French recipe. Ambitious in the kitchen, that's me.

I'm worried about Arthur. He's not an outside boy—
pale compared to his classmates.
Maybe he'll be an actor. This week he's pretended to be a lion-tamer,
an astronaut, a pirate and a bomb-defuser.
He puts on all these accents.
Practises in his bedroom with the door closed.
Last week I left a scouting brochure on Arthur's desk.
Yesterday I found it in the bin.

This morning at breakfast Arthur asked Damien
whether a bomb-defuser earns *heaps* of money.

Damien suggested that Arthur ask Uncle Des
as he's knocked around the world a lot and may know.

Enough about me and mine, Glenda. Tell me more about Gordon. You said he was a builder. Handy is good.

Observations and suggestions
- for Alfred Schnittke

A puddle is water relaxing.

The middle rungs of ladders don't get the credit they deserve.

It's hard to get an octopus to try on a jacket.

The one-winged bird may peck the hardest.

Don't get used to being used.

Look at what you do for a living and at what living you do.

Tide report

Wendy, our youngest, is sometimes so contrary it makes me seethe,
but I don't want her scared of me like I was of my Dad.
It was a relief when he went out to sea,
off the coast of Norway or down around the Canary Islands.

I did like it when he came back with a gift, an oceanic souvenir—
a whale bone, a shark's tooth, the dried tailbones of a stingray.

Nervy. Volatile. That was Dad. He'd witnessed young lads
swept overboard during storms. Back on land he'd often be
the one to knock on a cottage door, inform the parents.
Once he'd performed that duty, Dad would sit hunched over
at the kitchen table, rub at his face with his hands, then start stabbing
his food and tell us that we didn't understand *anything*.
Mum would take away his unfinished plate, start washing the dishes
at the sink, tell me and Carl to go and do our homework.

Poverty worried Dad more than storms. He learned to fix things—
kettles, toasters, sewing machines. All from repair manuals
which arrived in the post from London.
Word got around and he started to get customers.
Widow Jenkins was the first. He fixed her Singer—
it needed a new belt and some oiling.
She paid him in potatoes. Half a sack of them.

I'd see Dad sitting at his workbench—watch him insert
a new element in a kettle, then pause, look out the window
at the sulky Atlantic and I'd know he'd push off soon with his kitbag.

It was good then to see Mum less jumpy, more relaxed.
Inviting women friends around. They'd talk about
projects—making new curtains for the sitting room,
enrolling in a French correspondence course…
and Carl and I would start on a jigsaw puzzle,
maybe one of the Lake District.

Poem to the snail

I see you, on your slow commute
to the office of a leaf…

I like the way you carry yourself.
When you halt
it's to linger rather than loiter.

You try to keep a step ahead
of the pedestrian…

Should you be crushed
may this poem console you
with the assurance that the next rain
will lure others of your pace
out into the open.

Abundance

After brushing her teeth Wendy uses the toothbrush
to brush Spank the poodle's ears.
'Not all germs are bad,
some make me glad…' Wendy sings
until she hears Mum's footsteps on the stairs.

'Well, first day of the school year.
Don't forget your pencil case.
There's a slice of cheese and spinach pie
in your lunchbox.'

Margaret stands on the dusty edge of Carmel Road,
waves to the receding school bus.

Wendy, her youngest. No fits for a year now. Not
since the divorce. The house cleansed of Damien, the
furniture he broke,
the crystal sugar bowl thrown against the kitchen wall.

Piano lessons have resumed. Wendy's diligent.
Debussy. Ravel. Grieg. Lilt and trill.

Margaret walks along the fence line
to where the blackberries grow.
Sweetness among the thorns.

At the dentist

You may find out
that not every tooth likes its neighbour.

The words

Freed from the stable of the dictionary
they gallop across the plain of the poem.

What a poem is
for Jenny Bornholdt

A poem is more jazz than recipe,
more breast milk than formula.

A poem is daily life
or an inky break from daily life.

A poem is the glad yellow of lemons.

A poem is an odd sock made into a hand puppet.

A poem is medicine which tastes better than you'd imagined.

Sometimes it's a big breaking wave
effervescent around your driftwood bones.
Sometimes it's a big blundering wave that flattens your sandcastle—
so you start on another one.

Acknowledgements

Some of these poems, or earlier versions of them, have appeared in the following magazines and journals either in print form or online:

Antipodes (USA); *Glossen* (USA); *Meniscus*; *One Sentence Poems* (USA); *StylusLit*.

Thank you to:

Helen Bakowski and Ophelia Bakowski for sharing their love, patience, skills and valued opinions which make my daily and creative life richer.

Vera Di Campli San Vito for her friendship and for opening and easing introductions to the W Tree community.

Fred Koch and Neroli Hadfield of Ontos Farm for their friendship, knowledge, advice, stories, cups of tea and singing.

George Pados, Kirsten Harper, Sandra Jackson and Anise Clarke, staff, volunteers and residents of SIBA Retreat Centre for their friendship, enthusiasm, meals, massages, goat education and the rental of Jambala Cottage in 2021 and 2022—three stints there enabled me to realise the environments and atmospheres necessary to specific poems in *Our Ways on Earth*.

Mark Lelliott of NGS Global, for his friendship, generosity, support and annual poetry commissions, in subject matter I may not have addressed without the impetus and challenge each commission provides.

The owners, managers and staff of The Paperback Bookshop, 60 Bourke Street, and The Hill of Content Bookshop, 86 Bourke Street, for their kindness, conversations, generosity of spirit and for continuing to stock, sell and promote my poetry books.

Ken Bolton for his valued friendship and astute poetry advice.

Ophelia Bakowski again for the insightful cover photography and design. (www.opheliabakowski.com)

Andrew Bott for the author photo and our walks and talks together. (www.andrewbottphoto.com)

I specialize in reading my poetry in private houses, to groups of eight or more anywhere in the world. For further details contact:

pbakowski54@gmail.com   Mobile: +61 406 029 578

About the author

A bounding deer in the long grass of poetry, Peter Bakowski's poems continue to appear in literary journals worldwide.

In this century, Peter and his partner Helen, a clothes maker and textile enthusiast, have undertaken funded and self-funded creative residencies in Berlin, Macau, Suzhou (near Shanghai), Labastide Esparbaïrenque (near Carcassonne), Greenmount (near Perth, Western Australia), Battery Point, Hobart, at the Arthur Boyd estate, Bundanon, New South Wales, and on the Greek island of Skopelos.

In 2021 and 2022 they have undertaken self-funded Gippsland residencies in W Tree and Port Albert— each residency enabled Peter to write poems which he couldn't have written without the firsthand experience of the residency.

When not travelling, Peter, Helen, Buzz (an inspirational miniature black poodle) and Ophelia (who also has travel and creativity genes) are usually found strolling in the Fitzroy and Edinburgh Gardens and browsing in bookshops, record shops and fabric shops in Melbourne.

www.ingramcontent.com/pod-product-compliance
Ingram Content Group Australia Pty Ltd
76 Discovery Rd, Dandenong South VIC 3175, AU
AUHW020721050325
407891AU00005B/29

9 780645 180879